Getting Started

Quick Guide to Become a Self-Published Author

A Quick Approach to Rapidly Creating Materials for Publishing and selling through various outlets.

Getting Started
Quick Guide to Become a Self-Published Author

Chavonne D. Stewart

Dogwood Farms Publications

Copyright© 2019 Chavonne D. Stewart
All Rights Reserved
Published by Dogwood Farms Publications
Cover Art by Chavonne D. Stewart

Edited by Lisa Lickel
www.LisaLickel.com

No part of this publication may be reproduced, distributed or transmitted in any form or by any means, including photocopying, recording, or other electronic or mechanical methods, without the prior written permission of the publisher, except in the case of brief quotations embodied in reviews and certain other non-commercial uses permitted by copyright law. Thank you for respecting the hard work of this author.

Published in the United States of America
Adult/Self-Help

Paperback ISBN: 978-1-7338206-2-2
Electronic Format ISBN: 978-0-9863128-9-2
Library of Congress Control Number: 2019909712

Contact info: PO Box 2598 Acworth, GA 30102
www.chavonnestewart.com

Driven by the desire to help others and people asking my advice on how to get started with self-publishing process, I decided to compile a guide that would provide you the essential steps needed to get started. Also, I have included a few resources to consider to help bring your dream of being published into reality.

Acknowledgements

Thank you to all my family and friends who have supported me through the years. A special thanks to the rising entrepreneurs I have inspired... Never lose Hope, Have the Faith to believe that Dreams do Come True. Put Action behind your faith.

Table of Contents

Acknowledgements ii
Introduction 1
Section One: Writing 101 3
    Step One: What is Your Goal? 4
    Step Two: What is your topic? Be clear 5
    Step Three: Develop Your Outline 6
    Step Four: Pen to Paper 8
    Step Five: Writing Schedule 10
    Step Six: Create an Environment 12
    Step Seven: 3-Part Process…Write, Rewrite, then Refine 13
    Step Eight: Talk to the Professional 15
Section Two: Get Published 16
Section Three: Resources 19
About the Author 21
Other Books by Chavonne D. Stewart 22

Introduction

Today marks a life changing event in your life. You are about to have a major impact on individuals across this globe. How, you ask? You have decided to write your compelling story and share your knowledge. As soon as a thought enters your mind, "who," "what," "when," "where" and "how" questions take over. I can honestly say I have been in your shoes. My journey to becoming a self-published author took 30 years. Did your eyes get big? Did the words "huh" come out of your mouth? That's okay. My reaction was the same. I knew I wanted to tell this one particular story but, I didn't know how to begin. I had the meat of the story but I needed to build around it. There is a thing called "life." As life took over, my dream of writing the story was put on the back burner, not a forgotten but on a temporary hold.

One day I looked up and the market crashed. Life took a turn for the better. I am no longer employed so I have the time to write. My creative juices begin to stir up. I started the process of developing my first children's book. I had the character already, chose a name and decided on the premise of the story. Since the premise was like an adventure, I decided that in the entire series the characters would go on adventures but teach kids valuable lessons. Here are a few questions you can consider during the development process of your book.

Getting Started

- What qualities do I want my character to portray?
- What did I want my character and/or characters in the book to look like?
- What would be their personalities?

These are just some small details you have to consider when writing. My ideas were flowing like a river. I am overjoyed that the process had begun. In the midst of the writing, I started my research on publishing.

As you will learn, there are two options, traditional publishing vs. self-publishing. At the time I began my research, all I found were overly expensive options. The cost didn't line up with what was in my purse at the time; however, I didn't allow the cost of publishing to stop me from writing. I wrote multiple drafts until I was satisfied with my first story.

Once I reached that point I hit another standstill. Remember, I said earlier this was a 30-year process.

Finally, in 2014 my life changed for the greater. A dream was fulfilled. I became a self-published author. How? You may be wondering. As mentioned earlier, the cost was the reason I couldn't publish, but, I believe the saying "you have not because you ask not." You can't accomplish your dreams without the help of others. I started a new job and reached out to another person who had written and published. The basis of this book is to give you the information given to me as well as to help you think about your project in more depth.

Section One: Writing 101

Now your journey is beginning. It's time to develop your idea and put it on paper. Before you begin your journey be sure you have a journal because the brain dumping will start. Journals are not that expensive. You can even get the old fashion composition book. Now that you have everything you need including pen or pencil let's start the process. I gave you a little help below. I call this a guide for a reason, because I have provided you with eight steps to complete your first book as well as tips on publishing. Use your journal to answer questions in each step.

Getting Started

Step One: What is Your Goal?

Are you writing for fun, or to promote your business? Remember your main focus is serving and/or reaching your reader. Don't make the goal about money. You are in a learning process and your desire is to write a professional well-written product. Your focus on the writing will help you fulfil your goal. Jot down your ideas below.

Step Two: What is your topic? Be clear

A clear goal helps you to start thinking about the topic of the book. In my case, I knew the topic of my first book. I had to work on the development of the story. Are you writing non-fiction or fiction? Ask yourself what you are trying to communicate or teach with your book. Streamline your topic making sure you are not too broad. This will allow you to share much more relevant information about your topic with your reader and gives you the opportunity to write additional books related to the topic.

If you're writing fiction, which is what I have written so far, be sure you create your story and characters around a narrative that you know something about or have a passion for. The narrative for my story was based on real life experience.

What is your area of expertise? If you are a history buff or science guru, you could write a novel surrounding an idea from that subject. Maybe your writing goal is work related or related to your business. In doing so you could potentially create an anchor for various ideas you may have about your body of work.

Step Three: Develop Your Outline

To be honest with you, this is an area I have always struggled in even when I was in school. I have always jumped right into writing my papers. For whatever reason I thought I couldn't function well with an outline.

Recently, an idea came to mind about a book. Since I had read another book regarding outlining I said let me try it. I felt good afterwards because I could see my chapter book in a new light. I could target which area I would start to write first instead of being all over the place. So I want to encourage you to develop an outline. You can do one that is set-up like a table of contents. Or create an Octopus design with center body, eight arms and subheading arms. You should have at least an introduction, chapter headings, and conclusion. Whichever way you decide, just do it!

Getting Started

Getting Started

Step Four: Pen to Paper

Once you have a completed outline, it's time to develop the outline into actual paragraphs. Book formation begins. Ask yourself, which word processing software will I use? If you have Microsoft word, be sure you have the ability to edit your work. This doesn't mean you skip having an actual editor. We all need a system of checks and balances. Two heads are better than one. You also need to have your body of work formatted correctly. Be sure what ever process you use allows for easy editing.

    Side note, you can always start the old-fashioned way by using pen and paper. I do it all. I like to see my process of development over time. What are your thoughts on outline? Have you decided on your method? I recommend you do some research and write some notes below.

Getting Started

Step Five: Writing Schedule

Let me start by saying, I truly believe any person can write a book, manual, magazine article, etc. within 24-72 hours. I think it depends on how eager you are and if the creative juices are flowing. I have seen it happen and witnessed it for myself. We all have responsibilities in life that can hinder the writing process. I want to encourage you to keep a journal with you at all times. That way when ideals come to mind, you can jot them down. As far as a writing schedule, you have to determine the best time of day for you. I am a late night person because I like when the house is quiet. I can sit and just pour out my ideas. You may be the early morning person or mid-day.

Whatever time of day, allow yourself as much time as possible to just write. There are 7 days in a week; I recommend you write for at least 4 of the 7 days. Do you know it only takes you about 20-30 minutes to write 200 words? Think about it. 200 words a day for four days will be 800 words and for four weeks in a month that is 3200 words. You are on the way to completing your book.

Now that idea is on the smaller scale and you can definitely do more. But it's a start. So one of the things I want you to write below is your goal to committing to writing. Be specific about how many days, what time of day, how long and how many words you expect to write within the allotted time. Finally, utilize your calendar and alarms on phones as reminders of what you should be doing.

Getting Started

Step Six: Create an Environment

Ask yourself, what is the best place to work within the home? What spot do you think will motivate you the most to write? Pick out your best spot that you feel is conducive as well as most comfortable for writing. Think of your spot as a private sanctuary. It could be your office, just a desk, your kitchen table, or it may be outside on your covered patio. Wherever it is, personalize it with your special items. You may post a vision board to remind you of your goals. Music could be important to you as well as cathartic. You may need sustenance such as coffee, tea, juice or water to help create that environment for writing. Once you have decided, stick to it. Don't change. Jot down the area in your home and time of day you have decided to commit to writing.

Step Seven: 3-Part Process...Write, Rewrite, then Refine

Let me begin by saying, "NO CRITIQUING!" In anything that you step out to do, you can tend to be too critical of yourself. In this section of the guide, your main purpose is to complete the manuscript. Constantly reviewing and critiquing can stall the writing process. JUST WRITE! Write consistently and continuously. Let writing become a habit. There is a rule that says you can break any habit after 21 days however, in my opinion, that same concept can be used to acquire a good habit.

Once you have completed the manuscript in its entirety then you can shift to the rewrite process. You can do as many rewrites as you want. Each book I wrote has many drafts. Be sure you put a date on everything. It's a good way to track as well as view your progress. With each rewrite editing is taking place.

The greatest feeling you will get in this process is a finished book. Once you have completed your book draft, set it aside for a few days or a couple of weeks. This is the time when you need to refresh, revive and renew your thinking. You've been so close to this project while writing it that you need to create some distance. Then go back and read over the entire book again correcting mistakes, rewriting sections as necessary, cutting out wordy parts, and tightening it up. Take out words and passages that aren't absolutely crucial to the story or message. You may go through this process a few times.

    Don't give up. Refinement is the final step before you shift to Step 8. Refining the manuscript means you're removing all unwanted parts or any impurities that are hindering the flow of your manuscript. You want to get to the point that you feel pretty good about what you have written. Based on what you learned through this step, what your thoughts? Write them below.

Step Eight: Talk to the Professional

I am not saying you aren't a professional. If you recall earlier, I said two heads are better than one. You need four eyes to truly dissect your work. An editor is someone who you should be able to establish a long lasting relationship and a person who isn't bias but, will review your work objectively. An editor's job is to make sure the book flows properly and coherent. That person should verify if the usage of words is correct. A great editor polishes and refines the book for publication. Editors should check your facts; verify headings, footnote entries, and more. Editor should be able to determine if the work of fiction is logical. Editing is a massive process that should be done. Don't skimp or even skip the editing process. It could make or more than likely break you. Don't be cheap make the investment. Editing isn't free. You should always strive for excellence by releasing professional work. No editing can lead to bad reviews and could damage your credibility as a writer. Your work is a representation of who you are.

    Take a moment and write down/research potential editors you can contact.

Section Two: Get Published

First and foremost, I don't want cobwebs to build on your manuscript or for it to linger in your file folder on your computer. Your writing is meant to have an impact on others. The only way that can happen is for you to get published then promote through marketing and speaking events, etc... Don't worry about if you have a written a New York Times best seller. If it's meant for you to be one, you will be. With every book you write and publish, you'll learn more and become a better writer. You'll be inspired by other writers as you research and read more about writing and publishing. We all have to be a beginner before we become an expert. But the more you write the more of an expert you'll become. Our focus at this moment is to get the manuscript in a book form.

Once you get your first book published under your belt the next one will be a piece of cake. I am a living witness. There are no words to express the enthusiasm I have for this section. Even this day, four years later, I remember hitting the submit button to finalize my publishing process. I am a self-published author. My dream became a reality. When you go to Amazon or Barnes and Noble, my book titles will appear in paperback and eBook format. I have the same goal for you. I believe if you follow the steps in this guide, you will have that same sense of accomplishment. Eventually, I went from wanting to tell one story to having published three books in a children's series.

Getting Started

So how did I get there? Let me tell, things had changed since I first researched publishing options. I stepped out of my comfort zone and asked the questions. I was fortunate to work with a young lady who had published part of a book series and I believe she was working on book 4 or 5 at that time.

So I asked her the name of her editor and what company she publish with. She shared two words with me CreateSpace*. I had never heard of the company. She explained that CreateSpace is an entity of Amazon which offers a print on demand option. This means there are no upfront costs. Amazon gets their money from the sales. "Wow," I said to myself.

I knew I was in the right place at the right time. I pushed the envelope by asking about her editor. In that moment, I knew who I would publish through as well as having a potential editor. Sometimes people aren't willing to divulge information out of fear of someone doing better than them. The way we advance is through networking and sharing. I am glad she decided to share with me.

Next, I reached out to the editor. She was also willing to offer her advice as well. She had published several books. I learned how to purchase my own ISBN numbers. CreateSpace, or what is now Kindle Direct Publishing, can assign ISBN numbers but I chose to own my own. I researched the Library of Congress and how I can obtain a number for my books. Illustrations were needed for my story, and I was referred to a company that has many graphic artists to choose from at great rates. I was given everything I needed by being in the right place and asking the important questions. Finally, the last suggestion given to me by the editor was to create a publishing company name for my books. That's why I use Dogwood Farms Publications on all my materials. Eventually, I could decide to start helping others publish through my company. If I do so, I can do the necessary steps to form the company.

    In the resource section I have given links for you to review to aid in your process. The sole purpose of this guide is to provide you with a simple format to get your creative juices stirring. In the end, you will be a successful self-published author.

*NOTE: CreateSpace has been folded into Kindle Direct Publishing.

Section Three: Resources

As promised I have provided some links to help you through the process. I recommend you read through your links carefully before making decisions. Our steps may be the same but what works for each of us can be different. Most important is that you get to the finish line with a well thought-out book that is on the shelves of as many bookstores and eBooks as possible.

See next page for links to help you through the process.

Getting Started

Print on Demand Opportunities	Amazon : https://kdp.amazon.com/en_US/ Formats: EBooks & Paperback Ingramspark: www.ingramspark.com Formats: EBooks, Paperback & Large Print Hardback Kobo: www.kobo.com Smashwords: www.smashwords.com Format: EBooks **Other options:** Outskirts Book Baby Lulu
Graphic Designers	www.fiverr.com www.freelance.com
Editor Research	http://www.janefriedman.com/how-to-find-an-editor/ https://www.thecreativepenn.com/2018/03/30/how-to-find-and-work-with-a-professional-editor/
ISBN	www.bowker.com
Library of Congress (Number)	http://www.loc.gov/publish/pcn/

About the Author

Chavonne D. Stewart is a native of Atlanta, Georgia. She is an accomplished self-published author of the children's book brand, called *The Adventures of Amilya Rose*. In addition to her writing Chavonne is the founder of Chavonne Stewart Ministries International (CSMI). CSMI is built on the foundation of God's Word in Philippians 1:6: *He that began a good work*. At CSMI, we believe we have a responsibility to educate, empower, and embrace the next generation of leaders. Our goal is to develop leaders who will have an impact globally as **Ambassadors for Christ** (II Corinthians 5:20). We will achieve this goal through teaching, training, motivating, and mentoring singles to live for their purpose. In addition to serving in ministry, she is the CEO and Founder of *Living 4 Purpose Coaching*. Our goal is to help you *Refocus, Redefine* and *Reposition* yourself to *See Beyond Your Now*. We explore the strategies and support structures you need to succeed to make your dreams a reality. Chavonne received her training as a life coach through DreamReleaser Coaching, LLC. Currently, Chavonne is working on her PhD in Philosophy of Leadership Studies. She is an associate life coach and received her training through DreamReleaser Coaching, LLC. She holds a MS in Management and BA in History. She enjoys family/friend time, writing, traveling, DIY shows and shopping. She is the eldest of three.

Other Books by Chavonne D. Stewart

In Him Affirmations (May 2019)

The Adventures of Amilya Rose: Father-Daughter Dance (2016)

The Adventures of Amilya Rose: Disappearance (August 2015)

The Adventures of Amilya Rose: The Lie (February 2014)

www.ingramcontent.com/pod-product-compliance
Lightning Source LLC
Chambersburg PA
CBHW061349040426
42444CB00011B/3154